Classical Economic Principles & the Wealth of Nations

Book I: Classical Principles

Robert Genetski

Published by FastPencil, Inc.

Published by FastPencil, Inc.
3131 Bascom Ave.
Suite 150
Campbell CA 95008 USA
(408) 540-7571
(408) 540-7572 (Fax)
info@fastpencil.com
http://www.fastpencil.com

First Edition

This book is dedicated to my grandchildren—Alex, Jordon, Mikaela, Ellie, Catie, Adelai, Kaelyn, Dan and Ryleigh. May the knowledge and work of your generation serve to advance the spiritual and material well-being of mankind.

Contents

Introduction

At the turn of the 21st century the application of certain classical principles in China and India has helped to lift hundreds of millions of people from conditions of abject poverty... the greatest antipoverty program in history. At the same time, developed nations have abandoned some of these same principles. This has contributed to pockets of poverty and economic hardship in the midst of plenty.

It has been more than two and a half centuries since Adam Smith wrote *The Wealth of Nations*. Smith's objective was straightforward: identify and explain ideas and principles that would produce the highest living standards for the greatest number of people. He and those who followed in his wake provided a prescription for creating widespread prosperity. The prescription involves key *classical* principles... principles that are as relevant today as ever before.

Classical principles stem from a belief that each individual has God-given rights to liberty and freedom. These rights mean that so long as their actions do not harm others individuals must be free to pursue their own self-interests, without interference from an oppressive authority. Under such conditions, not only do individuals benefit from their own decisions, but those decisions benefit others, as well.

The history of the past two centuries provides conclusive proof of the power of classical principles. Time and again these principles have served as the keys to unlocking the wealth of nations.

Classical economists established a logical explanation regarding the creation of wealth. They presented evidence to support their views and made predictions based on the evidence.

Adam Smith used this approach to make seemingly astonishing forecasts. He predicted free market policies in the American colonies would eventually lead to greater wealth and prosperity than existed in England. He also predicted higher taxes and an oppressive government would prevent Spain's colonies in South America from developing as rapidly as the American colonies. Although he was ridiculed for such predictions, they proved to be accurate.

Others who followed classical principles have made equally astonishing predictions. The greatest economic success story of our time is China. In the late 1970s China was a poor country, unable to feed its people. Since then, the country's growth has been extraordinary. During the first decade of the 21st century China surpassed Japan to become the second largest economy in the world. At its recent rate of growth, by 2020 China will replace the US as the world's largest economy.

In the early 1980s, my good friend, mentor and fellow classical economist, Beryl Sprinkel visited China in his capacity as President Reagan's Under Secretary of the Treasury. When he returned he was bursting with optimism over what he had encountered.

"Bob, you won't believe what I saw there," he told me excitedly. "Upon entering the offices of every key Chinese official, I noticed their bookshelves were lined with classical economics textbooks. And when I met China's leader, Deng Xiaoping, he pointed to those books and told me, 'These guys got it right. These are the policies we will adopt. It will take time, but China will become the most powerful economy in the world.'"

In a single generation, Deng Xiaoping's prediction is about to be validated. While China still has a long way to go in implementing classical principles, its progress since the late 1970s has been extraordinary. China's experience is simply one small piece of evidence of the potential power associated with these principles.

It might seem that a topic as important as the creation of wealth should be fairly straightforward. It isn't. Every economic issue is steeped in controversy. The more significant the issue happens to be, the greater the controversy that surrounds it. There are reasons for this. Anyone interested in understanding economic issues and the accompanying controversies should be aware of these reasons.

To begin with, economics isn't the type of discipline that lends itself to absolute proof of a particular concept. To some extent, each economic experience is unique.

Time and again we might observe freer markets, lower tax rates and less government spending being followed by periods of strong growth and widespread prosperity. In contrast, we might witness that increases in government spending, regulations and higher taxes are followed by disappointing economic conditions.

In spite of what may appear to be an obvious conclusion, we can't have absolute proof that either set of policies caused the subsequent events. Such proof would involve turning back the clock and running the same conditions over with different policies.

Since we can't do this, anyone can claim the conditions that followed certain policy changes were not related to those policies.

Such claims are inevitable because economics involves important, emotional topics. Economics deals not only with the creation of income and wealth; it deals with how income and wealth are distributed. Every change in economic policy has implications for how much income and wealth will be created and for how it is distributed among individuals, groups and businesses.

All living things instinctively react when threatened. In the same manner, individuals, businesses and groups react to defend their interests. This natural defense mechanism, along with the impossibility of proving anything, provides fertile ground for disagreements over the causes and effects of every economic policy regardless of the evidence.

We can't prove that the classical principles that so captured Deng Xiaoping's imagination caused China's growth anymore than we can prove that the accuracy of Adam Smith's predictions was due to the validity of his principles.

Economists who disagree with the classical view can always respond, "Just because the Chinese had classical textbooks doesn't mean they read them. After all, we have the same books and we haven't read them."

Proof is illusive. In economics, we can only reason and observe. Since absolute proof is impossible, we must do the next best thing and look to the weight of the evidence. I maintain the evidence is so overwhelming it should lead most reasonable people to conclude that classical principles represent the keys to creating both wealthy individuals and wealthy nations.

Regardless of how pervasive the evidence is, there are those who will reject it. Those who believe that certain policies threaten their intellectual or financial interests will continue to defend those interests. It is their right to do so. However, others should recognize their opposition for what it is—a barrier to advancing the material well-being of mankind.

Economists have spent more than two centuries unraveling the mysteries behind the basic forces at work in the economy. For most key issues, appropriate explanations have been clearly and effectively presented. The underlying principles presented here are neither new nor unique. They draw on the work of many brilliant thinkers who labored extensively to hone and refine the ideas behind the creation of wealth.

Economic success and failure are two sides of the same coin. The game is rigged. We control the outcome. Pursuing classical principles promotes success. Rejecting them promotes failure.

The objective of this book is to provide a clear explanation of classical principles and the logic and reasoning underlying these principles. Subsequent books will show how following the classical path leads to economic success while failing to follow it leads to economic failure.

Classical economists provided a successful formula for creating the greatest wealth for the greatest number of people. Understanding their concepts and adopting their vision remains essential to fulfilling their primary objective—enhancing the wealth of nations by advancing the material wellbeing of individuals throughout the world.

CHAPTER 1

Origins of Classical Thought

We hold these truths to be self-evident, that all men are created equal, that they are endowed by their Creator with certain unalienable rights, that among these are life, liberty and the pursuit of happiness.—US Declaration of Independence

The term *classical* means different things to different people. To many, it refers to a specific period of time. People, ideas and accomplishments from that era are all painted with the same classical brush.

My use of the term is different. While the essence of classical thought emerged more than two centuries ago, many of the ideas and implications have since been developed and refined. What makes the ideas *classical* is not the era they came from but their very nature. They are *classical* because they are so basic and so fundamental that they are timeless.

Liberty and freedom form the basis for classical principles

Classical thought stems from a belief in the rights of mankind to liberty and freedom. The 17th century English philosopher John Locke traced these rights to their Judeo-Christian roots. Locke argued that God gave each man and woman equal rights to liberty and freedom.[1] Since these rights come directly from God, no person or government can take them away.

Locke's view ran counter to the tide of history. Throughout history people with wealth and power have tried to dictate how others should live. The Founders of the United States rejected this concept. They studied Locke's arguments and agreed that individuals had God-given rights to liberty and freedom.

First and foremost, liberty implies freedom from an oppressive authority. But true freedom involves something more. It means that individuals are free to pursue their own self interests, so long as doing so does not harm others. The Founders took the concepts of liberty and freedom and used them as the foundation for what became the greatest and wealthiest nation on earth—the United States of America.

Early classical economists and those who followed their path began with the premise that all individuals have an inherent right to liberty and freedom. They studied history in an effort to understand how people responded to particular circumstances. They observed human nature and how people tended to behave.

Both human nature and man's inherent right to liberty and freedom form the basis for classical economic principles. Since neither of these precepts change over time, ideas based on them are universal. They apply to all people at all times.

The primary objective is to raise living standards

The primary objective of the early classical economists was to help improve living standards for the vast majority of people. Adam Smith, the most prominent classical economist, was particularly concerned with the well-being of workers and the poor.

Smith's theories and prescriptions concerned economic growth. He knew that in order to raise living standards it was necessary to identify and promote policies that would best generate and sustain economic growth.

As with other classical economists, Smith abhorred waste and inefficiency. He did so out of concern that waste and inefficiency would undermine the living conditions of the working class and the poor.

Early advocates of classical thought saw free markets as an extension of individual freedom. They did not assume that markets were, or ever would be, perfectly free. Rather, they concluded that the more freedom people had to respond to market forces, the more efficient the economy would tend to be. And, the more efficient an economy became, the more its workers and the poor would tend to share in the benefits.

As a group, the early classical economists recognized that government was essential to any civilized society. However, they tended to distrust government, as well as powerful individuals and other established groups.

The distrust of the establishment stemmed from the classical view of human nature. These economists believed that people tend to act instinctively to further their self-interests. While the pursuit of self-interests would tend to contribute to the general welfare of all, there were exceptions. Established groups could use their money and influence to promote their self-interests at the expense of others.

So long as the government's power and influence were limited, established interests were less likely to be able to influence its policies. However, the more powerful the government became, the more these groups could be expected to spend their time, energy and resources to promote self-serving policies. Such favoritism would be at the expense of those with less political clout, namely the middle class and the poor.

In spite of the potential to raise living standards, many view a society based on self-interest as one driven by selfish behavior. They assume that individuals pursuing their own interests will have little concern or compassion for others and that those in need would suffer. Early classical economists believed that the opposite was true. The more wealth individuals produced, the more resources would be available to help the poor.

Nothing could change the innate desire of individuals to provide first and foremost for their personal needs and those of their immediate family. However, once those needs were met, individuals had a moral obligation to help the poor and others who were less fortunate. In a free society, this moral obligation resides with each individual, not with some oppressive authority.

Early classical economists responded to this moral obligation. They often took positions based on principles. Many argued for policies they believed would benefit society, even when such policies were not consistent with their own financial interests. They gave generously and anonymously to friends and those in need.[2]

The belief that all men and women have God-given rights to liberty and freedom has important implications. These implications involve certain principles and policies. It is inevitable that the principles and policies that flow from God-given rights must be those that provide the greatest material well-being for the greatest number of people. God wouldn't have it any other way.

CHAPTER 2

Basic Prinicples

History is the discovering of the constant and universal principles of human nature. —David Hume

Dramatic changes occurred in the latter part of the 18th century. The feudal system and agricultural economy gave way to the industrial revolution.

Prior to the industrial revolution understanding the economy was fairly easy. A workforce consisting of farmers and craftsmen was fairly easy to understand. Each person had a specific, easily understandable job. Most produced a finished product. Anything that was produced over and above what the worker needed was exchanged for finished products produced by others.

In the 17th century something new emerged. Machines replaced manual labor. Workers became less inclined to produce finished products. They instead became specialists, producing some part of a product.

Unlike the simplicity and order of the feudal system, the emerging system was chaotic. The pace of business increased dramatically. Then, as now, great changes led to great confusion.

Who should make key economic decisions?

In the feudal system, many decisions about production and distribution were made by a central authority. In the system emerging out of the industrial revolution, no one appeared to be in control. It was unclear just who would decide issues that were essential to fulfilling the needs of society.

What should be produced? How much of it? Who would produce it and how would it be produced? What would things be worth and how much should workers be paid?

There was confusion over how these crucial tasks could conceivably be accomplished without the aid of some central authority. People wondered how it would be possible to serve the nation's interests without someone in charge of such critical decisions. Logic seemed to suggest that the end result would be chaos.

Adam Smith carefully studied the emerging system. He noted the lack of a central authority. He recognized the seemingly chaotic interplay of forces at work and reached a startling conclusion.

Within this seemingly chaotic system were the keys to creating the greatest amount of wealth for the greatest number of people. Individuals, freely going about their normal business and free to pursue their self-interests, would tend to promote the interests of society far more effectively than when guided by any central authority.

The keys to prosperity were not to be found in the decisions of some powerful, enlightened leader. Nor were they to be found in the guidance provided by a council of wise men or politicians. Such powerful authorities were more likely to undermine prosperity than promote it. Rather, the key to prosperity resides in the interaction of free individuals responding to their everyday needs.

Smith's conclusions led to some basic principles that would enable nations to take full advantage of the wealth-creating potential of their people. These principles included an important role for government. However, instead of directing economic activity, government's role was to ensure that individuals were provided the optimal environment in which to maximize their creative and productive energies.

With the right environment, individuals would combine resources in the most efficient way possible to provide things that other people wanted. The characteristics of a productive environment could be distilled to four essential principles:

Promote free markets.

Keep tax rates low and limit the role of government.

Protect individual property rights.

Provide a stable currency.

Each of these principles flow directly from a belief in each individual's God-given right to liberty and freedom. As with liberty and freedom, the principles are so basic and fundamental that they apply to all people at all times.

Classical economists believed that these principles contained the keys to creating wealth. They had good reasons for these beliefs. We now turn to the reasoning behind each of these principles and examine why they are considered to be so important toward advancing the wealth of individuals and hence the wealth of nations.

CHAPTER 3

Free Markets

Any attempt to control prices or quantities of particular commodities deprives competition of its power of bringing about an effective co-ordination of individual efforts, because price changes then cease to register the relevant changes in circumstance and no longer provide a reliable guide for the individual's actions.—Friedrich A. Hayek

Free markets refer to a system where the prices and quantities of the things we buy and sell are unencumbered by artificial barriers or constraints.

The logic underlying free markets is straightforward. Whenever individuals agree to a transaction, they benefit from the exchange. Otherwise, they wouldn't agree to it. Hence, the free exchange of goods and services benefits those individuals directly involved.

In addition to benefiting those directly involved, the free exchange of goods and services also benefits others. As a general rule, the more markets respond freely to the forces of supply and demand, the more individuals are able to use the nation's resources efficiently to produce the things people want. Using resources efficiently contributes to the wealth of nations.

Making efficient use of resources is challenging. It requires a massive amount of information, cooperation and effort. Free markets provide the essential mechanism to accomplish this task.

Markets are extremely complex

We often take things for granted. When we buy something, we seldom give much thought to how it got there. When markets are free to operate just about anything we may want is almost always immediately available, as long as we are willing and able to pay the price.

Providing goods and services to the people who want them, when they want them, at a price that most are willing to pay is one of the most complicated tasks imaginable. It involves hundreds of millions of people making billions of decisions. Each individual contributes a small part to the process.

Grasping the complexity of the market system is the first step toward understanding why free markets are so crucial to creating wealth. An essay written over half a century ago provides some insight to this task.

Writing from the perspective of a pencil, Leonard Read makes the seemingly outlandish claim that there is not a single person on the face of the earth who knows how to make something as simple as a pencil. After explaining in great detail how the actions of millions of people all over the world contribute to the production of each component of a pencil, Read states:

...There isn't a single person in all these millions, including the president of the pencil company, who contributes more than a tiny, infinitesimal bit of know-how. From the standpoint of know-how the only difference between the miner of graphite in Ceylon and the logger in Oregon is in the type of know-how. Neither the miner nor the logger can be dispensed with, any more than can the chemist at the factory or the worker in the oil field—paraffin being a by-product of petroleum.

Here is an astounding fact: Neither the worker in the oil field nor the chemist nor the digger of graphite or clay nor any who mans or makes the ships or trains or trucks nor the one who runs the machine that does the knurling on my bit of metal nor the president of the company performs his singular task because he wants me. Each one wants me less, perhaps, than does a child in the first grade. Indeed, there are some among this vast multitude who never saw a pencil nor would they know how to use one. Their motivation is other than me. Perhaps it is something like this: Each of these millions sees that he can thus exchange his tiny know-how for the goods and services he needs or wants. I may or may not be among these items.

There is a fact still more astounding: the absence of a master mind, of anyone dictating or forcibly directing these countless actions which bring me into being. No trace of such a person can be found. Instead, we find the Invisible Hand at work.[1]

The *invisible hand* is the market system—a system that is so complex that no one individual knows how to make even the simplest product. It challenges the imagination to think what it takes to produce a TV, computer, or cell phone.

The complexity of creating anything of value is compounded by the fact that the entire system is dynamic. Our preferences are constantly changing. So is our knowhow and technology. Each change reverberates through the system affecting the supply and demand for all resources. These changes in turn affect each and every component of each and every product.

The challenge facing producers is daunting. If they fail to make all the proper decisions they will produce products that are too expensive to sell or are unsalable for any number of other reasons.

Producers must continually incorporate massive amounts of information and adjust production and delivery processes to assure that resources are continually used in the most efficient manner to produce the things that people want.

Only the invisible hand of a market system can coordinate the process to accomplish this task. It does so through the miracle of the price system. The price system provides all the information necessary so individuals can make the most efficient use of all available resources to provide us with the things we want.

Free markets make efficient use of resources

When prices are free of artificial barriers and constraints, they tend to reflect the relative scarcity of resources. A high price signals a product or resource that is relatively scarce compared to its demand. The high price not only informs everyone that this item is valuable, it also signals precisely how valuable it is to each person.

How much we have to spend often reflects what we have been paid in exchange for our knowhow. We use that knowhow to produce things that others want. What we choose to buy depends on our financial resources and our preferences. Each of us is unique. Each of us has a different amount of money to spend. And each of us attaches a different value to the things we want.

The market system is the only system that enables each of us to know precisely how much of our knowhow (in the form of money) we will have to give up in exchange for the things we want. The price of anything we want captures this vital information about our individual choices. Our response in either buying or not buying certain things at certain prices feeds this information back to producers. They then respond to our choices.

We all adjust to prices. We do this without needing to know why the price is higher or lower. In fact, the beauty of the free market system is that it isn't necessary to have all the information regarding what causes a high or low price or what causes it to change. The price itself contains all the information we need to make efficient choices.

At higher prices we have to exchange more of our money to get the item. Those with sufficient money and a great desire to have the item may pay the higher price. Others decide either to use less of the item or substitute something else. We adjust our purchases to reflect the value that each item has to us.

Lower prices indicate that the item is relatively plentiful compared to the demand.   Armed with such information, each of us responds in a way that best fulfills our own unique preferences.

Similar decisions are made by producers.   They use the price system to decide which products to make, which resources to use, whether to substitute machines for workers, or whether to use a foreign product or service instead of a domestic one. As with individuals, the price system provides producers with all the information they need to make the most efficient decisions in each of these areas.

Our labor is the key resource used to create goods and services. In a free market, hard-working, conscientious workers that contribute to creating more value tend to get paid more than lazy, less conscientious workers. This encourages workers to be more productive and discourages them from being less productive.

Rewarding wise decisions and productive behavior while penalizing poor decisions and unproductive behavior promotes efficiency. The resulting distribution of income tends to place more resources and responsibilities in the hands of those who are more responsible and more productive. At the same time, it tends to shift resources away from those whose behavior is less responsible and less productive.

The more individuals and prices are free to respond to market pressures, the greater will be the tendency for a nation to use its resources efficiently. A failure to appreciate the importance of free markets undermines the entire wealth-creating process.

Alternatives to Free Markets

The principal alternative to a free market system involves government officials substituting their judgment for the free market price or quantity of various items. These officials would have to decide whether a price should be higher or lower than the market price, or whether more or less of some particular product or resource should be used.

In doing so, officials replace the unique collective preferences of all individuals with either their own preferences or the preferences of those who lobby for such changes.   The end result rewards some and penalizes others based on the opinions of certain select individuals.

Altering the free market price of any resource reverberates through the economy affecting countless other prices. By distorting the entire system of prices, such decisions tend to produce an inefficient use of resources.

Once we grasp the complexity of the market system, it becomes readily apparent that no authority is capable of understanding the system. No authority could conceivably possess even a small fraction of the information necessary to make the type of decisions that are made unconsciously by those responding to market forces. Hence, no authority can be capable of making the type of choices necessary for generating and sustaining wealth. Adam Smith put it this way:

The statesman who should attempt to direct private people in what manner they ought to employ their capitals, would not only load himself with a most unnecessary attention, but assume an authority which could safely be trusted, not only to no single person, but to no council or senate whatever, and which would nowhere be so dangerous as in the hands of a man who had folly and presumption enough to fancy himself fit to exercise it.[2]

In a free market system government has a specific and important role to play. That role is the topic of Chapter 8. For now, it's important to understand that when government officials impose their preferences over those of the market, they curtail individual freedom. And in the process, they distort the information necessary to provide for the efficient use of resources.

It is for all these reasons that early classical economists believed that giving individuals more freedom to respond to free market forces would tend to promote the wealth of nations.

CHAPTER 4

Objections to Free Markets I: Inadequate Wages

The high rate of unemployment among teenagers, and especially black teenagers, is both a scandal and a serious source of social unrest. Yet it is largely a result of minimum wage laws. We regard the minimum wage law as one of the most, if not the most, anti-black laws on the statute books. — Milton Friedman

Classical economists view free markets as a system that best allows us to satisfy our unique individual desires. It does this by responding to our preferences while providing the information necessary to produce the most efficient use of our resources.

Many believe that there are serious problems with free markets. Some claim that in the real world markets aren't really free; that they provide excessive rewards to the rich; punish the poor; promote an inequitable distribution of income; are disruptive; and are responsible for volatile economic conditions. Others point out that free markets cannot provide certain public goods nor protect us from monopolies and unscrupulous behavior.

Concerns regarding public goods, health and safety, and unscrupulous behavior are legitimate. However, failures that critics ascribe to free markets are often failures of government to perform its legitimate responsibilities. Classical economists never assumed government should absolve itself from those responsibilities. The legitimate responsibilities of government and its contribution to creating wealth are discussed in Chapter 9.

The other critiques of free markets are troublesome because attempts to alter market outcomes tend to be destructive. Such attempts don't just limit the creation of wealth; they often impoverish the very individuals the critics presume to help. This chapter deals with one of the most serious and most destructive objections to free markets—that it impoverishes certain workers. The following chapter deals with various other critiques of the free market system.

Free markets fail to provide for an adequate wage

This criticism of free markets is particularly disturbing. The classical case for free markets is that they serve to increase opportunities and living standards for the poor. Nonetheless, some critics claim that markets impoverish the very people they are supposed to benefit.

Critics usually claim that one solution to low wages is to pass laws mandating that certain workers receive higher wages. The idea that government can determine the value of certain workers' services involves a serious misunderstanding of economics.

Anyone with the most rudimentary knowledge of business knows that a company can control either the price of its product or the quantity it will sell. It can't do both. If it chooses to alter the price, the market will determine how much it will sell. If it wants to sell more, it usually will have to lower the price.

When government sets a minimum wage above the market, fewer workers get hired. It's as simple as that. The higher the minimum wage is above the market wage, the more lower-skilled workers are priced out of the job market. Imposition of a so-called "living wage" is among the cruelest and most damaging of all government policies.

The US first established a minimum wage with the Fair Labor Standards Act of 1938. President Roosevelt characterized the Act as "the most far-reaching, far-sighted program for the benefit of workers ever adopted in this or any other country."

While such noble comments are often associated with minimum wage legislation, many of its original proponents had something different in mind. They were well aware of the economic consequences of placing a minimum wage above the level determined by market forces.

Many early reformers favored instituting a minimum wage, not to raise the living standard of low wage workers, but to reduce the number of what they referred to as "undesirable" workers. In his epic historical analysis of the progressive movement, Jonah Goldberg notes,

It was ...(a) belief, shared by many of the progressive economists affiliated with the American Economic Association, that establishing a minimum wage above the value of the unemployables'

worth would lock them out of the market, accelerating their elimination.[1]

No one today openly claims to favor a "living wage" as a means of literally destroying the families of low-wage workers. The arguments for the minimum wage have changed. The economics have not. The damage these laws do to individuals and their families is as destructive as ever.

A digression

Permit me to digress with a personal story. We often view things in the context of our personal experiences. Such experiences can have a lasting impression on the way we view the world.

A wave of immigrants inundated the United States in the early part of the 20th century. Among this wave was Olga Chernovsky. Olga was my grandmother. She came to this country, as many did at the time, with nothing but the clothes on her back. She couldn't speak the language, couldn't read or write. This helps to explain how each of her children ended up with a different version of the family name.

As a young boy I was fascinated by Grandma Olga. I vividly remember her stories about conditions in the Ukraine where she was born. "We were desperate for work," she would say in that harsh, heavily accented Eastern European voice.

"Life was hard, very hard. We often walk five, ten miles to find even a bit of work. Even when we find work, pay was almost nothing. Too often, there was no work."

Then, her eyes began to sparkle. Her face lit up with excitement as she talked about her first experiences upon coming to the United States. Although she had no skills and couldn't speak the language, there was work.

"I could not believe," she said excitedly recounting those memories, "I had all the work I wanted. And I wanted work. I work one job all day. At night, I work a job. On weekends, I work again. I love it. For me, this is paradise. "

Fortunately for Grandma Olga, and very likely for the history of my family, there were no minimum wage laws in the early 1900s. Market forces determined wages. Employers were free to pay workers what their services were worth for the job at hand. Workers were free to decide whether or not the pay being offered was worth their effort. This was a free market.

It's hard to imagine anything more personal and more basic than the freedom to make an agreement concerning your own labor and time. This right no longer exists. The US government (as do all but a handful of state governments and many governments around the world) now dictates the minimum wage that a person must be paid.

Had today's minimum wage been in effect at the beginning of the 20th century I have no doubt Grandma Olga would have been priced out of the market. She may well have sat home, idle and demoralized.

The same people who would have claimed that they were protecting Olga from being paid less than a living wage would no doubt feel sympathy for her plight. They would probably insist that government programs be established to provide her with food stamps, unemployment compensation and other forms of welfare.

Olga would have hated it. She was a proud, independent, hardworking woman. She had found her worker's paradise. For her, her work and enjoying the fruits of her own labor made life worthwhile.

Taking her paradise away and replacing it with welfare would have made her a dependent of the state. The dependency may well have reverberated through our family for generations to come. We can never know what might have been. What I do know is that Olga's work ethic was passed down to my parents and to me. I believe I can see that same work ethic in my children and even in my grandchildren.

Today's ghettos are filled with families less fortunate than mine. These are families whose history was influenced by government attempts to fix a perceived flaw in the free market. Setting a minimum wage priced many of their family members out of jobs. A lack of jobs led to more government policies designed to help these families. Instead of helping, the policies contributed to a dependency that undermined the dignity of many in these families. The real flaw wasn't with the free market. It was with the failure to allow the market to operate.

Minimum wage laws harm the most vulnerable workers

There is no doubt about the damage a minimum wage can do. Just imagine what would occur if the legal minimum wage were set at $24 an hour. Workers who contributed less than this amount to their firm's bottom line would lose their job. At least half the workers in the US would be priced out of jobs. If the legal minimum wage were set below this lofty level, fewer jobs would be lost. The lower the minimum wage is set, the fewer the number of workers who are priced out of the job market.

Since it was first imposed in the US in 1938, the federal minimum wage (in today's dollars) has ranged from a low of $3.60 an hour at various times in the 1940s to a high of $10 an hour in 1968. The average has been $6.75.[2] With the minimum wage in this range the effect of the law has been mainly to price those with the lowest skills and the least job experience out of the job market. It's instructive to look at groups that have tended to include a large proportion of such workers and to compare their unemployment rates both before and after the introduction of the legal minimum wage.

Prior to the 1930s there appear to be no significant differences between the unemployment rates for the total labor force and those for teenagers or blacks.[3/] After the imposition of the minimum wage in 1938, the unemployment rates for teens, blacks and particularly for black teenagers have risen dramatically above the rates for the total labor force. In an extensive analysis of unemployment in America, Vedder and Gallaway note:

Further examination of the evidence suggests the large racial differential in unemployment rates had its genesis in the 1930s and 1940s, with an additional aggravation of that difference in the 1970s. While Americans often pride themselves on reducing racial economic distinctions over time, the evidence on unemployment is highly inconsistent with that sanguine interpretation.[4/]

From 1948-2010 the unemployment rate for the entire US labor force has averaged 5.7%. The average for teens has been almost twice this total. For black teenagers the unemployment rate has averaged 29%, more than four and a half times that of the total labor force.

It's discouraging to see jobs destroyed by misguided government efforts to raise wages. Programs designed to help people by imposing arbitrary wage requirements may have the noblest of intentions. However, such intentions cannot account for the fact that each individual is unique. Each of us is uniquely qualified to determine whether working for the wage we may be offered is worth our effort. No one else is qualified to make that judgment.

Workers priced out of the job market by the minimum wage tend to be among the most vulnerable of all workers. They are often young, first-time workers who desperately need the valuable experience that can only be acquired from on-the-job training. They may also be those with learning disabilities who need additional supervision, training and patience before being able to make a productive contribution.

There are many ways to assist the most needy and vulnerable workers while maintaining each person's freedom and dignity.[5] Setting a minimum market wage is not one of them. Even when a government imposes a minimum wage so low that it doesn't affect anyone's wages, it remains a destructive force. It does so by implicitly telling people that it is not their individual talents, but the government that determines what they are paid. This is a cruel and deceptive message that can serve to undermine the self-esteem of vulnerable workers.

By permitting government to control something as deeply personal as the value of an individual's services, we implicitly concede the most personal of all our freedoms—the price of our own services. As with so many attempts to interfere with free markets, there are serious, unintended consequences to relinquishing that freedom.

CHAPTER 5

Objections to Free Markets II: More Objections

A major source of objection to a free economy is precisely that... it gives people what they want instead of what a particular group thinks they ought to want. Underlying most arguments against the free market is a lack of belief in freedom itself. — Milton Friedman

There are certain objections to free markets that may sound reasonable at first blush. However, upon closer examination, their substance quickly dissipates. Here are a few:

Free markets aren't really free

Some suggest that free markets are fine in theory, but that perfectly free markets don't exist in practice. This is true. The real world is filled with imperfections. However, the rationale for efficiency doesn't require that markets be perfectly free. It merely posits that the more freedom there is for prices and the quantities of items to reflect the pressures of supply and demand, the more efficient the system will tend to be.

Free markets provide excessive rewards to the rich

Free markets do provide substantial rewards to certain individuals. Microsoft's Bill Gates is a prime example. One *New Yorker* cartoon featuring two people in conversation reads: "I hated Bill Gates before it became so fashionable."

Many people envy the rich. Those that do often believe wealth is fixed. They believe the "haves" have it at the expense of the "have-nots."   In the words of P.J. O'Rourke, they consider wealth to be like a pizza. The more others eat, the less there is for me. And if others eat it all, I'm left eating the box.

The idea that wealth and income are fixed is simply wrong. Wealth and income are dynamic. Innovative people are always figuring out ways to increase the amount of pizzas and anything else that people want. When they do, the market rewards their innovation.

Major innovations enable all types of businesses to increase their efficiency. The benefits spread to the whole population. When businesses using the new innovation become more productive, their customers, workers and owners all benefit.

In a free market economy, innovators tend to receive benefits in direct proportion to the number of those who benefit from the innovations. This was the case with Bill Gates and Microsoft.

Rather than resent rewards to those whose contributions increase the material well-being of others, we should celebrate their achievements. Their rewards are an integral part of a natural system that tends to direct income and wealth toward those who do the most to advance the material well-being and living standards of others.

In this sense, the free market system reflects the universal law. The greater the contribution individuals make to the material well-being of others, the greater the material rewards they tend to receive for their contribution.

Limiting the rewards for innovations limits innovations. In so doing, it limits the material well-being of all who stood to benefit from those innovations. The idea behind increasing the wealth of nations isn't to make the rich poor, but to make the poor rich.

Even so, there are many who resent the generous pay packages often available to those who run businesses. Few seem to realize that only a portion of that compensation is due to the influence of their decisions. A relatively large portion of a chief executive's pay represents the ultimate reward that incentivizes many others to strive to achieve that position.

As with so many aspects of market behavior, the rewards and penalties associated with a CEO's job performance are far more complicated than they might at first appear to be. Owing to this complexity, attempts to rearrange market compensation in line with someone's perception of "fairness" are more likely to destroy wealth than create it.

Nonetheless, there is little doubt that some receive rewards far beyond their contribution. This is true whether markets are free to operate or are controlled by government.

In fact, what may well be the most egregious example of compensation abuse occurred with the government-created, government-sponsored agencies Fannie Mae and Freddie Mac. Mismanagement of these entities not only contributed to the overall financial crisis in 2008, but analysts estimate that the total cost to taxpayers from bailing out just these two agencies will eventually be close to $700 billion.[1/] The key executives who were instrumental in the failure of these agencies walked away from the wreckage with pay packages ranging from $20-$50 million.[2/]

To the extent that compensation abuses occur in a private, free market setting, a company's directors and shareholders bear the responsibility. This is as it should be since it's their money. When government is involved in compensation abuses, it's the nation's taxpayers who foot the bill.

Free markets produce an unfair distribution of income

Some critics of free markets believe that they lead to an unfair distribution of income. These critics seem to believe that no one should earn too much or too little. The previous sections show how replacing free market outcomes with concepts of fairness not only places limits on freedom and growth, but can also impoverish individuals.

A related complaint is that under free markets the difference between the incomes of the rich and poor is greater than some believe it should be. Even though free markets may increase living standards for all income groups, some claim that the poor may *feel* oppressed when others have so much more than they have.

This is an elitist complaint. Elitists seem more concerned with the feelings of the poor than with their material well-being. Those who experience poverty first hand are far less concerned with feelings and flawed statistical analysis than with improving living standards for themselves and their families.

As US living standards soared in the latter half of the 20th century, the gap between the living standards of the lowest paid workers in the US and those in most underdeveloped countries also soared. Statistically speaking, the gap between those with nothing and those whose living standards are improving must always be increasing.

One notable factor contributing to the gap between the rich and poor in the US is immigrants. Those coming to the US from underdeveloped countries tend to dramatically improve their material well-being. However, since their US wages tend to be relatively low, their presence lowers the country's *average* wage. Those who complain about declining living standards and the widening gap between the rich and poor often seem oblivious to basic statistical facts. A nation's average living standard can decline even while the living standards of all its groups are increasing. Moreover, living standards of *all* groups can be increasing at the same time that the gap between the rich and poor increases.

Statistics regarding the economic well-being of a nation's population can be confusing even to economists who should know better. Interestingly, these statistical quirks were something that Will Rogers readily grasped. To paraphrase the great American humorist, "When the Beverly Hillbillies left the Ozarks and moved to Hollywood, they raised the average intelligence level in both states."

Free markets are disruptive

Free market critics witness factories shutting down, workers losing jobs, communities suffering. They see foreign products replacing domestic products and families struggling. Their conclusion is that when bad things happen, free markets must be responsible. However, when economic conditions change, markets react. The reaction in markets reflects the changes and complexities associated with any economic system. By reacting, markets adjust so that resources can continue to be used efficiently in the new environment.

The US economy is among the most dynamic in the world. Each year the economy loses roughly 30 million jobs. In a good year, roughly 32 million new jobs appear.[3] Even when there is no change in the total number of jobs, there are tens of millions of new jobs created and lost.

The normal dynamism of a market economy is what contributes to an efficient use of resources. It is the key to raising living standards for the vast majority of people. Not everyone experiences these benefits. Businesses and workers that are either unable or unwilling to adapt to changing conditions lose out. Poor profits, losses, lower wages and layoffs are often signs of a failure to adapt to changing markets.

It makes no difference whether the competition comes from other domestic producers or from foreign producers. The effect is the same. Businesses and workers that fail to adjust to changing conditions experience problems.

The alternative to having markets adjust is to have government officials override market signals. Politicians or bureaucrats would have to decide which prices, wages, or products should avoid responding to market pressures. They would then have to offer their own ideas regarding the most appropriate prices, wages, and myriad other inputs provided by free markets.

Such decisions can appear to promote stability. They may temporarily save certain jobs. When they do, the stability comes at a cost. By failing to adapt to changing conditions, the productive process becomes progressively less efficient. When that happens, any temporary gains to workers directly affected come at the expense of all other workers.

The longer market pressures are ignored, the more painful the inevitable adjustments become. The greatest and most painful job losses occur where companies, unions or government policies prevent a response to changing market conditions.

Promoting inefficiency undermines the productive power of any economy. In so doing, it undermines both the value of the country's output and the wages earned by its workforce. Failure to adjust to changing economic conditions is a sure road to impoverishing any nation.

Free markets encourage price gouging during emergencies

Over half the states in the US have laws prohibiting charging "excessive" prices during an emergency. The public is often outraged when businesses use such emergencies to boost prices.

What is often ignored is that price gouging during emergencies is the market's efficient way of dealing with a difficult situation. Noted economist Thomas Sowell explains why even during emergencies, free markets provide a superior solution to economic problems than one that artificially constrains prices:

Among the complaints in Florida is that hotels have raised their prices. One hotel whose rooms normally cost $40 a night now charged $109 a night and another hotel whose rooms likewise normally cost $40 a night now charged $160 a night.

Those who are long on indignation and short on economics may say that these hotels were now "charging all that the traffic will bear." But they were probably charging all that the traffic would bear when such hotels were charging $40 a night.

The real question is: Why will the traffic bear more now? Obviously because supply and demand have both changed. Since both homes and hotels have been damaged or destroyed by the hurricanes, there are now more people seeking more rooms from fewer hotels.

What if prices were frozen where they were before all this happened?

Those who got to the hotel first would fill up the rooms and those who got there later would be out of luck — and perhaps out of doors or out of the community. At higher prices, a family that might have rented one room for the parents and another for the children will now double up in just one room because of the "exorbitant" prices. That leaves another room for someone else.

Someone whose home was damaged, but not destroyed, may decide to stay home and make do in less than ideal conditions, rather than pay the higher prices at the local hotel. That too will leave another room for someone whose home was damaged worse or destroyed.

In short, the new prices make as much economic sense under the new conditions as the old prices made under the old conditions. [4]

Many instinctively react with indignation at price gouging during emergencies. It appears obvious sellers are taking "unfair" advantage of a calamity to overcharge their customers. A more thoughtful analysis reveals something else...free markets providing the most efficient solution to allocating scarce resources at a time of distress.

Free markets lead to recessions and depressions

There is substantial evidence government policy mistakes have been responsible for every major peacetime recession over the past 90 years. Prior to every peacetime downturn in the economy, the

Federal Reserve moved to slow the creation of money.   Prior to the most serious downturns, including the Depression and the so-called Great Recession in 2008-09, the Federal Reserve actually reduced the funds available to transact business. A more complete analysis of the government's role in creating business cycles appears in Books II and III of this series.

Rather than attribute downturns in the economy to the irresponsible behavior of individuals or to a lack of regulations, it's instructive to study government policies. Those who do will find those policies are closely related to the economic hardships that follow.

It's important to recognize that many of the critiques of free markets are simply not valid.   Free market critics tend to ignore the fact that the alternative to free markets is bureaucratic manipulation and control. Upon closer examination it is apparent that most efforts to correct misconceived flaws in free markets not only reduce individual freedom, they also undermine efforts to promote wealth and prosperity.

CHAPTER 6

Low Tax Rates

*A wise and frugal government, which shall leave men free to regu-
late their own pursuits of industry and improvement, and shall not
take from the mouth of labor the bread it has earned - this is the
sum of good government. -Thomas Jefferson*

Early classical economists believed that taxing income, commerce
and wealth would limit the creation of each. Their reasoning is
straightforward. When you tax something, you get less of it. They
also believed in limiting the power and scope of government.
While low tax rates and limited government go hand in hand,
there are important reasons why each is essential to creating
wealth.

The importance of low tax rates was clearly spelled out over a
quarter century ago by Adam Smith:

*Every tax ought to be contrived as both to take out and to keep out
of the pockets of the people as little as possible, over and above what
it brings into the public treasury of the state. A tax may either take
out or keep out of the pockets of the people a great deal more than it*

brings into the public treasury in the four following ways. First, the levying of it may require a great number of officers whose salaries may eat up the greater part of the produce of the tax, and whose perquisites may impose another additional tax upon the people. Secondly, it may obstruct the industry of the people, and discourage them from applying to certain branches of business which might give maintenance and employment to great multitudes. While it obliges the people to pay, it may thus diminish, or perhaps destroy, some of the funds which might enable them more easily to do. Thirdly, by the forfeitures and other penalties which these unfortunate individuals incur who attempt unsuccessfully to evade the tax, it may frequently ruin them, and thereby put an end to the benefit which the community might have received from the employment of their capitals. An injudicious tax offers a great temptation to smuggling. But the penalties of smuggling must rise in proportion to the temptation. The law, contrary to all ordinary principles of justice, first creates the temptation, and then punishes those who yield to it; and it commonly enhances the punishment too in proportion to the very circumstance which ought certainly to alleviate it, the temptation to commit the crime. Fourthly, by subjecting the people to the frequent visits and the odious examination of the tax-gatherers, it may expose them to much unnecessary trouble, vexation, and oppression.... It is in some one or other of these four different ways that taxes are frequently so much more burdensome to the people than they are beneficial to the sovereign. [1]

Low tax rates also encourage the type of behavior we find most commendable. As parents, we have certain attributes we would like to see in our children. The most important of these are sound spiritual and moral qualities. In addition, most of us want our children to work hard to develop the knowledge and skills necessary for successful careers. We also want them to make wise decisions, be conscientious workers, spend money prudently and save for their future needs. Children learn from their parents. When parents act responsibly, children are more likely to follow their lead.

The greater the rewards for financially responsible behavior, the more individuals are likely to behave in a financially responsible manner. In so doing, their behavior not only benefits the individuals themselves, it provides an important lesson for others.

Low tax rates encourage work

Work is essential. Without it, nothing gets done. And yet, human nature is such that, given a choice, most individuals would just as soon not work. Adam Smith put it most eloquently,

It is in the interests of every man to live as much at his ease as he can; and if his emoluments are to be precisely the same, whether he does, or does not perform some very laborious duty, it is certainly his interest... to neglect it altogether.[2]

Human nature is such that the more money we offer for a certain task, the more likely it is that the task gets done. By the same token, the more individuals are allowed to keep the fruits of their labor, the more they will be inclined to choose work over leisure.

A hard-working, industrious citizenry is essential to a prosperous nation. When low tax rates enable parents to keep more of the fruits of their labor, it not only encourages them to work and produce more, it also provides a constructive example for children to follow.

Low tax rates encourage financially responsible behavior

While work is essential, it is not sufficient to increase living standards. To accomplish that it is necessary to become more productive—to produce more with less effort. To do so we must accumulate certain tools. These tools consist of such things as machinery, buildings, education, research and infrastructure.

Acquiring these tools involves a combination of sacrifice, risk and time. Sacrifice is the first step in the process. For most people spending money is easy. Saving it is difficult. Saving involves sacrificing current enjoyment.

Sacrificing current enjoyment provides the basis for creating more output. When people decide not to spend a portion of their income on current enjoyment, those funds are available to spend on tools that can increase future output. The more individuals decide to postpone current enjoyment, the more their earnings are available to create the tools needed for future growth.

Investing in the future involves substantial risks. Building machines and factories, conducting research, acquiring skills and creating infrastructure all take time. During the process a lot can change. Changes in tastes or preferences, technology or knowhow or any of a host of other factors can lead to tools that are obsolete or ineffective.

Anyone investing for an uncertain future can be disappointed in the outcome. They may lose the time, effort or money involved. Nonetheless, without those willing to accept such risks, it is impossible to improve living standards.

To some, the idea that low tax rates encourage the type of behavior essential to growth and prosperity appears obvious.

Upon graduating from college my daughter decided she would invest some of her salary in stocks. We discussed the merits of specific stocks. At the end of the conversation I happened to mention that she should be prepared to pay tax on any money she might make from selling her stocks.

She looked at me with a puzzled expression.

"Oh Dad," she said in a sweet, but somewhat condescending voice, "I'm sure you're wrong about that. There couldn't be any tax."

"Why would you say that?" I asked.

"Well, my friends and I are all working. We all paid taxes on what we earned, so what's left belongs to us. My friends choose to spend their money on CDs, vacations and all sorts of fun things. The government doesn't tax any of their spending," she explained.

"If the government doesn't tax frivolous purchases, it certainly wouldn't tax those who decided to sacrifice and take risks to improve their future. It doesn't make sense to penalize constructive behavior. That would be dumb. No one could be that dumb. Dad, I'm sure you're just so wrong about that tax."

And yet, in the US the federal government and most state governments tax both interest on savings and gains on investments. Taxing the income of those who choose to save and invest makes individuals more inclined to spend and incur debt. When individuals choose to engage in irresponsible financial behavior it not only limits future growth, it also provides a perverse example of destructive behavior that is passed on to future generations.

Low tax rates direct resources to more productive uses.

As previously noted, markets tend to reward people based on their contribution to creating goods and services for others. The extreme example of this is the much-reviled founder of Microsoft, Bill Gates. With its software, his company has been indirectly responsible for creating more goods and services for more people than any other company in history. In return for such an amazing feat, Gates was rewarded to the point where he became the wealthiest person in the world.

Gates made a number of very successful business decisions in Microsoft's early days. Those decisions helped its customers to become more productive. As its customers prospered, Microsoft prospered. Its earnings soared. In the company's early stages all of its earnings were plowed back into the business. Doing so led to further improvements.

The ongoing process of reinvesting funds into a successful business contributed to a progressively better product. This, in turn, produced a quantum leap in efficiency for the company's clients.

Since the client base involved all types of businesses throughout the world, the gains were multiplied many times over.

The combination of the market system and relatively low tax rates funnels progressively larger amounts of money to successful individuals and businesses—those that are most instrumental in increasing efficiency.

By enabling those who are successful to retain a greater portion of their earnings, low tax rates provide those individuals and companies with more resources to expand their success. In so doing, the entire economy becomes progressively more productive. This leads to greater wealth and higher living standards.

The alternative is to tax the type of behavior that promotes growth. Doing so shifts resources away from those with a proven record of efficiency and success. It either redirects those resources to government, with its proven record of inefficiency and failure, or to others who were apparently unable to compete successfully for private funds.

There is yet another way in which tax rates can misallocate resources. The higher the tax rate and the more complex the tax system, the greater will be the incentive to avoid or minimize tax burdens. To do so, there will be a growing demand for smart, innovative people to become tax lawyers and tax accountants. These occupations serve a valuable function for their clients and it's in the self-interest of people to pursue such work.

However, it is the high and complex tax system that creates an incentive for innovative people to use their talents to help shift potential tax dollars from the government back to those who earned them. In a simple, low tax system, the talents of individuals in these professions would be directed more toward creating wealth than redistributing it.

For all these reasons, high tax rates retard growth and prosperity. In contrast, low tax rates particularly those on savings and investments, promote the type of constructive behavior that leads to a wealthier nation.

CHAPTER 7

Limited Government

Man is not free unless government is limited. — Ronald Reagan

Early classical economists were concerned that a powerful, intrusive government would harm both individual freedom and a nation's prosperity. There are good reasons for this belief.

Intrusive governments reduce freedom

In his book *Private Rights and Public Illusions*, Tibor Machan provides an extensive analysis of how a powerful, intrusive government is inconsistent with a nation of free and independent people.

The desire to "help" others by directing their lives may be strong, but to yield to this desire is to undermine the very human dignity of the person who is being benignly coerced. In a society that accords with the principles based on the political theory of natural human rights to life, liberty and property ..., paternalism is not authorized. [1]

Government policies that treat people as dependents of the State undermine the independence and dignity of those they intend to help.

Powerful governments promote inefficiencies in the private sector

After studying human nature and history, classical economists concluded that individuals pursuing their own interests would tend to promote the interest of the entire nation. However, when government becomes powerful and intrusive, that same pursuit can undermine prosperity.

Established individuals, businesses, labor organizations and politicians each have their own interests. When government's responsibilities are limited, the potential of these established interests to receive special treatment is also limited.

As the scope and influence of a government expands, so does its ability to bestow favors on particular groups. Government can erect barriers to trade, pass specific tax breaks, adopt regulations and use any of a host of other means to reward certain groups.

The greater the power of government to grant favors, the more the established interests will devote time, effort and money to obtain special treatment.

Early classical economists believed that an expansive government was more likely to favor those with power and influence than those without power and influence. With a powerful, intrusive government, established interests would tend to use their resources to further their own interests. These interests involve adopting policies that direct the nation's resources toward those established interests. Such benefits would come at the expense of those without power and influence—the poor and middle class.

The larger and more intrusive a government becomes, the more it attracts a whole new industry of lobbyists and lawyers whose main function is to direct more of the nation's output to their clients. As in the case of tax lawyers and accountants, these professions attract smart, innovative people. They enter these fields to serve their own interests while performing a valuable service for their clients. However, with a limited, less intrusive government their talents would be redirected toward creating wealth rather than redistributing it.

Hence, not only does a powerful government tend to reward the "haves" at the expense of the "have-nots," but in the process the nation as a whole suffers. Since free markets promote a highly efficient use of resources, using the government's power to redirect those resources reduces a nation's total wealth.

Expansive governments need high tax rates

The more government's size and influence increases, the more it must tax its citizens to pay for its expanded activities. For all the reasons previously noted, high tax rates limit the rewards for productive activity. Hence, paying for a large bureaucracy also limits the creation of wealth in the private economy.

Governments tend to be inefficient

In addition to any damage it might do in the private economy, government tends to be inefficient in performing its own functions.   Private companies effectively perform the most complex tasks in an effort to provide individuals with the goods and services they want.

In contrast, government often has difficulty performing even the most basic tasks. Something as simple as counting people or votes often presents a significant challenge.

There are many reasons why government tends to be inefficient.

In the private sector, free markets contain an inherent mechanism to promote efficiency and limit waste. The mechanism automatically rewards success and penalizes failure. Profits measure a company's success in efficiently providing people with what they want when they want it. Losses measure a failure to do so.

Mistakes and poor judgment are a part of human nature. When they occur in business, companies lose market share. If mistakes continue, the company can go out of business.   Owners and workers all pay a price for bad decisions. Competitors who make better decisions reap the benefits.

In spite of severe penalties for failure, mistakes and poor decisions are inevitable. Even the best run companies experience problems. Through its system of rewards and penalties, the free market mechanism continuously works to promote efficiency and limit the impact of bad decisions.

Government has no comparable mechanism.   Rather than limit waste, the political mechanism actually promotes wasteful behavior. As in the private sector, mistakes and poor decisions are inevitable. The difference is that the public sector lacks a mechanism for automatically penalizing poor decisions or for holding anyone accountable.

Without the guiding force of profits and losses, politicians and bureaucrats need an alternative means to measure success and failure. The alternative tends to be the amount of money and resources used to achieve its objective.

Whatever the objective, the political mechanism tends to equate success with the amount of money it spends. When government programs fail to achieve their objective, the normal political response is to blame the failure on a lack of spending. Regardless of how many regulators or agencies have been created to deal with a problem, if the problem persists the normal political solution is to create more agencies, more departments, more regulators and more regulations.

The natural tendency for government programs to be wasteful is compounded by the fact that bureaucrats are spending other people's money. Human nature and numerous studies show that we tend to be more careful and efficient spending our own money than spending other people's money.

Furthermore, in the US the federal government wasn't designed to operate efficiently. Government was designed to provide rules and guidelines so that the individuals could operate efficiently. Given their concerns over the abuse of government, the Founders deliberately designed a system of checks and balances to diffuse power. This makes it difficult for the federal government to do anything efficiently.

A large and powerful government undermines true prosperity in many ways. It reduces individual freedom. It takes resources from their most efficient uses and reallocates them to those with power and influence. It raises taxes, thereby limiting productive behavior. And, since it lacks a mechanism to promote efficient decisions, government tends to waste a nation's resources in performing its own functions.

All of these reasons support the concerns of early classical economists regarding the role of government. To promote the wealth of nations, the power and influence of government has to be contained.

CHAPTER 8

Government Failure

Giving money and power to government is like giving whiskey and car keys to teenage boys. — P.J. O'Rourke

Previous chapters explain how government attempts to correct the free market have tended to create serious problems for the individuals directly affected as well as for the nation. There are sound reasons why government solutions tend to be inferior to free market solutions. The most important reason is that government solutions deprive individuals of their freedom and liberty.

Each of us is unique. Our choices and preferences are specific to our individual needs. In attempting to dictate wages, diet, health needs or any other aspect of our lives, government policies attempt to impose on us someone else's concept of what is best for us. To the extent government succeeds in doing so, we lose a crucial freedom—the freedom to determine our own needs, our own destiny.

Neither free market critics nor the government they rely on is capable of knowing what each of us needs to fulfill our pursuit of happiness. Such personal issues are unique to each of us. Free market critics undermine our freedom of choice as well as our ability to control our destiny when they assume they know what's in our best interests.

The fallacy of free market failures

The economic literature is filled with claims of free market failures. In each case, the critics have a unique way of defining success. Whether discussing wages, unemployment, credit, insurance, or the market for used cars, these critics conclude that markets fail whenever they do not achieve the critic's personal idea of perfection.[1]

The real world is imperfect. Classical economists never assumed that free markets were perfect. Rather, they assumed that they performed better than any real world alternative.

Suggesting that the free markets fail implies there is a superior solution. The only alternative solution to the free play of markets is to have government override the market. In order to conclude that markets have failed, it is necessary to show that government policies succeed in providing a superior solution.

The massive size and scope of government activities in the US and throughout much of the developed world is based on the assumption that government provides superior solutions to the market. Classical economists deny such an assumption. Rather, the classical position is that the vast size and scope of government activities undermines our freedom and our wealth.

The size and scope of government

The inefficiencies associated with government would not create much of a problem if government activities were limited. As the size and scope of government expands, its propensity for inefficiency expands.

In 2009 the US federal government spent $3.5 trillion providing services to its citizens. As part of this spending, there were more than 68 government agencies that regulate economic and social activity. Estimates suggest that the private sector spends over $1 trillion a year to comply with federal government mandates.[2]

In addition, state and local governments spent $3 trillion for their activities. There are no reliable estimates showing how much the private sector spends to comply with state and local mandates or how much state and local governments spend to comply with federal mandates.

Hence, in 2009 we could explicitly identify $7.5 trillion spent on government-related services. This amounted to roughly $60,000 per worker for that year. Since the income of all producers amounted to $12.2 trillion, government activities took over 60% of the nation's income. Individuals were left with less than 40% of their income to fulfill their needs.

Research indicates that the government's efficiency is roughly half that of the private sector.[3] This research suggests that government activity represents a massive waste of resources—a sum that amounted to roughly $30,000 per worker in 2009. Such waste raises fundamental questions regarding the efficacy of governmental activities.

Efforts to expand the role of government tend to be associated with the "haves"—those with large incomes and substantial assets. For the "haves," the perceived benefits of spending $60,000 a year for government programs can represent a relatively small portion of their wealth.   The "have-nots" seldom realize the extent to which the full cost of government programs reduces their incomes.   If they did, they would most certainly choose to reduce those programs.   Doing so would provide them with additional income to satisfy their immediate needs instead of having those resources go to government programs.

Government failures versus free market failures

Advocates for aggressive and expansive government assume that the political mechanism is capable of correcting the flaws they believe exist with free markets. However, the combination of the magnitude of government activities along with its noted inefficiencies suggests that any claims of free market failures have to be evaluated alongside government failures.

Interestingly, those who are among the most vocal advocates for expanding government's responsibilities are also those who are most disappointed in government's failure to accomplish its objectives.

In his book, *Free Lunch*, retired New York Times reporter David Cay Johnston consistently criticizes what he perceives as free market failures. He insists that government take more responsibility for correcting such problems. He then provides extensive evidence for the failure of the very governmental power he wants to expand.[4]

In one case, Johnston describes in great detail the emotional trauma suffered from the deaths on passenger train travel in the US. He provides extensive statistics to show how deadly this mode of travel has become. His solution is for government to provide better regulations and more regulators.

Curiously missing is the one solution that would not only have eliminated the deaths, but would also have eliminated significant taxpayer expense. That solution is the free market. Without governmental subsidies, passenger train travel would be much less common. All of the emotional trauma and tragedy Johnson laments would have been avoided had the free market been allowed to operate.

Regulating greed and speculation

Many people believe that the financial collapse in 2008-09 stemmed from greed and speculation. They insist that new regulations can prevent future problems.

Greed and speculation are basic characteristics of human behavior. They have always existed. They exist with or without free markets. The issue is not whether they exist, but whether they are likely to do more damage under a system of free markets or when government policies attempt to forbid or correct for such behavior.

It is widely acknowledged that government policies encouraged the behavior that contributed to the financial crisis of 2008-09. Government agencies—Fannie Mae and Freddie Mac—helped to promote and expand the market to securitize home mortgages. Government policy helped to undermine the value of those mortgages by encouraging lending to those with poor credit.

Many individuals did speculate in real estate. However, government policies clearly encouraged far more speculation and vulnerability than otherwise would have occurred. Not only did government policies encourage irresponsible behavior, but they did so at a significant cost to taxpayers.

The Congressional Budget Office estimates that between 2008 and 2020 the two government-sponsored agencies that help to finance the housing boom will cost taxpayers over $380 billion.[5] Updated private estimates late in 2010 place the total cost of these failed government agencies at closer to $700 billion.[6]

Following the Enron scandal in 2001, Congress enacted the Sarbanes-Oxley bill (SOX). In an effort to prevent fraud, the bill increased the role and responsibilities of the Security and Exchange Commission (SEC) while placing significant new financial burdens on publicly-held companies. As with all regulation, SOX was expensive. From 2003-07, US companies spent more than $50 billion to comply with the legislation.[7]

We may never know if this massive expenditure prevented any fraud. What we do know is that immediately after spending over $50 billion to prevent fraud, the regulations did nothing to stop the biggest private Ponzi scheme in history. Bernie Madoff's clients no doubt took comfort from knowing that the SEC investigated his firm twice and examined it on three separate occasions without finding any problems.[8] Without the SEC, Madoff's investors might not have been so trusting.

We also know that in spite of its huge cost, SOX failed to prevent the most significant financial crisis since the 1930s. Undaunted by this failure, the political process forged ahead with still another massive piece of legislation known as the Dodd-Frank financial reform. This bill contains more than 30 times as many regulations as SOX.[9]

Assuming compliance costs are similar to those under SOX, the new financial regulations would cost more than $1.5 trillion or roughly $11,000 per worker. As usual, the political process confronted failure by increasing the power and scope of the very regulatory apparatus that failed while handing the bill to taxpayers.

Regulating the environment

During the last half of the 20th century numerous laws were passed to prevent various forms of pollution. Rather than declare certain acts of pollution illegal, governments established regulatory agencies to oversee environmental issues.

These agencies have made significant progress in providing the US with a cleaner environment. However, as with other government activities, the regulatory agencies are highly inefficient. They are also subject to the influence of special interests.

The proliferation of government along with its numerous regulatory agencies, rules and regulations has become so great that it has actually promoted rather than contained pollution.

The oil drilling accident in the Gulf of Mexico in the spring of 2010 is a case in point. As it has in numerous other areas, the federal government adopted special incentives for companies to drill for oil. Government incentives are inconsistent with free markets. This is true whether the specific incentives are for research and development, exports, investment or anything else.

In addition to incentives to drill for oil, Congress passed laws limiting oil company liabilities with respect to accidents. Such limits on liabilities are also inconsistent with free markets. Potentially dangerous businesses should be liable for any damage they may do to others.

It is entirely possible that without government incentives and limits on liability, British Petroleum would have been less inclined to take the risks it took that led to the spill.

Nonetheless, accidents happen. In this case, it happened in spite of the existence of at least half a dozen government agencies and departments with responsibility for assuring the safety of those operations. As the following quote from a New York Times reporter indicates, the very existence of numerous federal departments prevented a response that could have limited the damage.

Under intense media scrutiny, at least a dozen federal agencies have taken part in the spill response, making decision-making slow, conflicted and confused, as they sought to apply numerous federal statutes....

Debates over the speed — or lack thereof — of the government response have also played out in Louisiana, where state officials spent much of May repeatedly seeking permission from the federal government to construct up to 90 miles of sand barriers to prevent oil from reaching the wetlands.

For three weeks, as the giant slick crept closer to shore, officials from the White House, Coast Guard, Army Corps of Engineers, Fish and Wildlife Service, National Oceanic and Atmospheric Administration and Environmental Protection Agency debated the best approach. [10]

When oil company executives testified before Congress they were asked why they weren't more prepared for dealing with a major spill. They explained that they were *required* by federal regulators to base their preparations on government models. Those models, prepared by the government's Mineral Management Services Department, gave very low odds of oil hitting shore, even in the case of a spill much larger than the one in the Gulf of Mexico. [11]

In this instance, the multiplicity of federal agencies, some of which were established to protect the environment, ended up permitting more environmental damage than would have occurred had those agencies not existed.

Free market critics tend to overstate government's potential to correct perceived flaws with free markets. They fail to acknowledge that flaws in the political process often prevent government from performing its legitimate role of protecting its citizens.

Government regulation and controls are fine in theory. In practice, they waste resources and promote irresponsible behavior. In so doing, they undermine prosperity. And, as with the minimum wage, bureaucratic controls rob individuals of basic freedoms while providing consumers with a false sense of security, all at a substantial cost.

Upon close examination one thing becomes readily apparent. Many of the recommended solutions to perceived flaws in the free market end up creating far greater problems than those they intend to solve.

It would come as no surprise to classical economists that established interests tend to co-opt government to enrich themselves. Nor would it come as a surprise that as the power of government has grown, so have the inefficiencies associated with that power.

This is precisely what those economists had warned against. They saw that the only workable solution was to limit the scope and power of government. Limiting government would limit the efforts of the establishment to use government to further its interests. It would also limit private sector inefficiencies that are an unintended byproduct of an intrusive government.

CHAPTER 9

Government's Role in Creating Wealth

According to the system of natural liberty, the sovereign has only three duties to attend to... first, the duty of protecting the society from the violence and invasion of other independent societies; secondly, the duty of protecting, as far as possible, every member of the society from the injustice or oppression of every other member of it... and, thirdly, the duty of directing and maintaining certain public works and certain public institutions, which it can never be for the interest of any individual, or small number of individuals, to erect and maintain.... — Adam Smith

Although they were concerned with the damage government could do, classical economists recognized that government plays an essential role in creating wealth. That role is to provide the necessary environment so that a nation's individuals can prosper and, in time, build a wealthy nation.

Government's primary responsibilities

Government has a number of essential functions. The most important of these is to protect its citizens from harm inflicted by others. In addition to providing protection from threats posed by foreigners, government has an obligation to protect its citizens from each other. To fulfill this responsibility government has to establish an effective legal system and provide the means to protect individual property rights, enforce contracts and provide appropriate penalties for those who harm others.

Critics tend to assume that under a system of free markets businesses and individuals are free to do whatever they want. The assumption is false. There is an essential qualification to the concept of freedom. We are free to do whatever we want *so long as our actions do not harm others.*

Harming others involves using force or coercion to compel them to do something they would prefer not doing. Harming others infringes on their freedom. It undermines their right to enjoy life, liberty and the pursuit of happiness. One of government's essential duties is to enforce this important qualification. Government is the only entity authorized to use force to discharge this responsibility. To the extent that individuals are permitted to harm others, it represents a failure of government, not a failure of free markets.

For example, no one has the freedom to defraud another person or take another person's property. Nor is anyone free to dump garbage in someone else's yard, or pollute the air or water to the extent that it harms other people.

With this crucial qualification, government's responsibility in a free market economy is to ensure that the prices and quantities of goods and services respond freely to the decisions made by individuals. Not only must government avoid artificially interfering with free market prices and wages, it also has a responsibility to ensure that others don't exert such power.

This means that first and foremost government should avoid using its coercive power to control prices and wages or to restrict trade. Furthermore, it means that government should avoid allowing businesses and labor unions to engage in such behavior. Businesses often lobby government officials to institute rules, regulations and tariffs that will restrict competitors and enhance their profits. Unions also lobby to impose tariffs as well as for laws that enable them to restrict the supply of workers so they can artificially boost wages and benefits for their members.

When powerful businesses and unions rely on government to prevent free markets from performing their proper role, the benefits flow to a privileged few. The costs are incurred by all others. Those with power and influence want to control markets for one purpose—to direct a greater share of the nation's resources to themselves than markets would allow. This occurs at the expense of those who lack power and influence. Restricting the free market limits both individuals' freedom of choice and the efficient flow of resources.

Misconstruing harm and injustice

Some free market critics urge government intervention wherever they perceive that some harm or an injustice has occurred. When wages are lower or higher than these critics think they should be, they conclude that some harm has been done. They also often see harm when businesses close and jobs disappear.

Those who perceive harm and injustice whenever things are not as they would like them to be do not believe in freedom. Rather, they want government to use its coercive power to substitute their own preferences for the preferences of others.

The role of government is to serve as an impartial referee. When a referee becomes an advocate for a particular group, it undermines the concept of justice. If a judge were to ignore the law and use his or her personal perspective to favor one side in a dispute, it represents a clear perversion of justice. In a similar manner, those who call upon government to implement their own personal concept of "justice" commit the real injustice.

In a free society, individuals and businesses are responsible for their own actions. They are free to do any number of things. They are free to take a risky job or do things that may endanger their own health and safety. Sky diving, competitive sports, smoking and eating unhealthy foods are risks that many individuals willingly take. A nation that chooses to decide what risks individuals can undertake is not a free nation.

P.J. O'Rourke best captures the concept of freedom when he notes that "America wasn't founded so that we could all be better.

America was founded so we could all be anything we damned well pleased."

Businesses are also free to take risks. In a free society they are free to produce inferior or cheap products, charge exorbitant prices and pay their workers and managers whatever they choose. As with individuals, the managers of those businesses must then take the responsibility and accept the consequences of their choices.

Consumers are also free to determine what products they will buy, what they will buy and who they will buy them from. And workers are free to determine who they will work for and what is acceptable compensation for their services. These are all characteristics of a free society.

In a free society, fairness is determined by the interaction of market forces. It is the result of free individuals choosing what they want without the coercive action of politicians or bureaucrats.

The proper role of government is to set the rules that apply to all and then enforce them. Placing restraints on free markets replaces the choices made by all free individuals with someone else's concept of fairness, justice or acceptable risk. When government changes the rules in such a way to help one group by hurting another it becomes a biased and corrupt judge.

There are many who benefit from government moves to override the free market. Those receiving benefits reward the politicians who are responsible for their gains. In contrast, those who are harmed by such decisions are often unaware that the referee has rigged the game against them.

Government does its best to promote freedom, liberty and prosperity when its rules do not reward some at the expense of others.

Public goods and available resources

As Adam Smith indicated, government can provide certain public goods more effectively than any individual or small group acting alone. The nature and extent of these public goods depend on various factors.

When living standards are limited, resources to provide public goods are also limited. As a nation's wealth increases, the scope of what are considered proper public goods will naturally tend to expand.

Environmental concerns are generally not a high priority when people are struggling to provide their families with necessities. Dealing with pollution becomes a high priority only after there is a sufficient increase in living standards. One of the many advantages of becoming a wealthy nation is that it enables individuals to enjoy more and better public goods.

Regardless of how wealthy a nation might become, the list of desirable public goods will always exceed its means to provide them. As so often occurs with individuals, there is a tendency for collective wants and desires to exceed available resources.

Prudent individuals limit their wants to a reasonable share of their resources. A prudent nation does the same. In order to grow and prosper and to promote individual freedom, public goods must be confined to a limited share of the nation's resources.

The case for limiting public goods is based on the concept of freedom. Each move to expand the scope of public goods reduces individual freedom and choice. A majority in the nation may want to expand the public sector and be quite willing to forgo its freedom in the process. However, doing so not only reduces the freedom of those in the majority, it also reduces the freedom of those in the minority who preferred their freedom to an expanded public sector.

In determining the scope of public goods it is important to note the tendency for a nation to produce more pubic goods than its citizens would prefer. In a democracy, a bias often exists because the benefits from many government programs are concentrated among relatively few people while the costs are widely dispersed.

The few who may benefit from a specific government program often find it worthwhile to spend time, energy and money to adopt the program. Conversely, there is little incentive for those who are forced to pay the relatively small per person cost of that program to expend a similar effort to oppose it.

This bias toward increasing government programs explains how they could expand to cost $60,000 per worker. For most workers, the cost of those programs far exceeds the income they have to meet their more pressing, personal needs.

In addition to this bias there is a tendency to underestimate the cost of public goods. The direct cost involves the resources individuals must give up to pay for the public goods. There are also indirect costs.

Once government has assumed the responsibility for accomplishing a task, individuals may feel less inclined to duplicate the effort. This can be particularly damaging since individuals and private organizations can be more effective than government in accomplishing various tasks.

The bias toward expanding public goods and underestimating their costs creates a serious challenge to limiting public goods to a reasonable share of a nation's economy.

Public goods and helping those in need

Early classical economists believed that every civilized nation had a responsibility to help those who were unable to help themselves. Free individuals are caring individuals. Many voluntarily use their resources to help those in need. However, if private means are not sufficient, there is usually widespread support for the public sector to assume that responsibility.

With substantial increases in wealth over the past two centuries, people have understandably insisted on expanding the nature and extent to which they believe government should help those in need. Laws providing for public funding of education or aid to children of parents who neglect their responsibilities involve helping those who are unable to help themselves.

A more complex issue is whether government should provide aid to those who are able to help themselves and choose not to. Taking money from one group to help others harms the former. Hence, redistributing other people's income is inconsistent with the principles of liberty. Using our own resources to help others involves true charity. Taking resources from some to give to others who are able to help themselves is not charity. It's stealing.

In addition to the implications for liberty, evidence suggests that government tends to be particularly inept in its efforts to redistribute income. Charles Murray provides an extensive analysis of how government welfare programs in the US harmed the recipients even more than they harmed those forced to pay for the programs.[1] One of the reasons for this is that chronic poverty is less associated with the possession of material goods than with a state of mind. By creating a sense of dependency and entitlement, government programs contribute to chronic poverty.[2]

Early classical economists believed in helping the working poor. Based on principles of liberty, they did not believe that others should be forced to pay for such help. Rather, they favored policies specifically designed to help low-wage workers.

Free markets were among the most important of these policies. Classical economists believe that a free market system is the most effective of all programs in providing the poor with greater opportunities to increase their material well-being. The greatest harm to the working poor comes from a powerful, intrusive government that uses its power to reward some at the expense of others. The others tend to be the working poor.

In addition, early classical economists believed that government should avoid taxing necessities. The main idea is to make sure that low-wage workers benefit fully from the fruits of their labor. While opposing income taxes in general, early classical economists would have been particularly opposed to taxing the wages of low-income workers, such as occurs with the payroll taxes that fund Social Security.

Public goods and efficiency

Whether a nation is rich or poor, government spending can make a positive contribution to achieving prosperity. To do so the spending not only has to be efficient, it has to be more efficient than the spending would have been had it occurred in the private sector. This presents a serious challenge. As noted earlier, government lacks a mechanism for achieving efficiency.

Building public roads to facilitate commerce can be a highly productive expenditure. However, if the roads aren't necessary or if they cost too much to build, the expenditure becomes wasteful.

A nation may have sufficient wealth that its citizens decide that everyone should have access to a certain basic amount of education and health care. While these are noble objectives, they pose significant challengers.

Markets are complex. Providing a system that efficiently provides for quality education and quality health care is a daunting task. For all the reasons noted earlier, government is not designed to accomplish such tasks.

Given the efficiency of markets, governments should rely on the free market mechanism to the maximum extent possible to accomplish its objectives. Using free markets to provide public goods tends to use the least amount of the nation's resources to provide the most benefits. In contrast, using the political mechanism to provide such goods tends to use the most resources to provide the least benefits.

Utilizing the efficiencies associated with free markets is clearly in a nation's best interests since it enables government to save resources that can be used for various other noble purposes.

Government efficiency—laws versus regulations

Even when performing its legitimate functions, such as containing fraud or controlling harmful pollution, the inefficiencies inherent in government can make a situation worse than it would have been without government action.

Problems occur when politicians fail to carry out their responsibilities. Those responsibilities consist of writing laws that clearly identify the acts that inflict harm on others. When a nation's laws are not clear, or when regulations produce a complex system of legal requirements, it creates the demand for a whole new industry of lawyers and lobbyists. Individuals enter these fields to serve their own interests. When they succeed they earn high incomes and provide a valuable service to their clients. However, their main contribution is to redistribute income from others to their clients. In a system of limited government and clearly defined laws the talents of these individuals would be directed toward creating wealth rather than redistributing it.

Effective lawmaking is a challenging task. It involves countless hours of detailed analysis, hard work and difficult decisions. Extensive committee hearings and discussion are usually necessary to define what constitutes a harmful act and what specific actions should be outlawed to prevent such harm. Finally, there is a need to provide guidance with respect to appropriate penalties or compensation for any harm that is done.

In the case of the environment, politicians would have to determine which specific pollutants inflict harm on others. They would consider the costs associated with limiting or eliminating those pollutants. Lawmakers might then weigh the harm done by those pollutants against the harm done eliminating them. They might also want to consider an appropriate period of time before a law takes effect so that technology and free markets can contribute to achieving the objective with the least amount of disruption.

Politicians avoid all this difficult work when they create regulatory agencies to do the work for them. Such an approach to lawmaking represents a dereliction of duty. Not only is the end result often ineffective, it's cumbersome, limits individual liberty and is prohibitively expensive. In short, it represents still another failure of government to operate in the interests of its citizens.

In his writings that shaped the Founders framework for establishing the US Constitution, John Locke explains the role of the legislature:

...The legislative cannot transfer the power of making laws to any other hands: for it being but a delegated power from the people, they who have it cannot pass it over to others. The people alone can appoint the form of the commonwealth which is by constituting the legislative, and appointing in whose hands that shall be. And when the people have said, we will submit to rules, and be governed by laws made by such men, and in such forms, nobody else can say other men shall make laws for them; nor can the people be bound by any laws, but such as are enacted by those whom they have chosen, and authorized to make laws for them. The power of the legislative

being derived from the people by a positive voluntary grant and institution, can be no other than what that positive grant conveyed, which being only to make laws, and not to make legislators, the legislative can have no power to transfer their authority of making laws and place it in other hands. [3]

Time and again critics believe they have discovered flaws in the free market system. On closer examination it appears that, to the extent problems exist, the failure rests with government and its inherent inefficiencies rather than with the free market system.

For all of these reasons, classical economists believe that low tax rates and limited government are essential to creating prosperity.

CHAPTER 10

Property Rights

The earth, and all that is therein ... belong to mankind in common...; yet being given for the use of men there must of necessity be a means to appropriate them some way or other, before they can be of any use, or at all beneficial to any particular man.

Though the earth...be common to all men, yet every man has a property in his own person: this nobody has any right to but himself. The labour of his body and the work of his hands...are properly his. Whatsoever then he removes out of the state that nature hath provided, and left it to, he hath mixed his labour with, and joined it to something that is his own, and thereby makes it his property. – John Locke

Low tax rates, a limited government and free markets are all essential to creating wealth. However, none of these factors would be meaningful without the rule of law to protect individual property rights. The failure to protect individual property rights will prevent poor countries from developing. And when property rights become less secure it will seriously undermine even the most prosperous economy. Property rights are the most basic of all the classical principles.

In establishing the US Constitution, the Founders relied heavily on the works of John Locke. Locke preceded both Adam Smith and the Founders by a century. He argued that every individual has an inherent God-given right to his or her property.

The great and chief end, therefore, of men's uniting into commonwealths, and putting themselves under government, is the preservation of their property.[1]

Locke, Smith and other classical economists believed that protecting an individual's right to his or her property was important both on moral and economic grounds. From the standpoint of morality, they believed that the property rightfully belonged to those who created it. However, they also believed that individuals who accumulated a sufficient amount of property over and above what they needed had a moral obligation to help those who were starving or who could not help themselves.

Those who wrote the US Constitution agreed to the importance of protecting property rights. James Madison pointed out there are inherent differences in each person's industriousness, skills and abilities. As a result, some would end up with property. Others would not. Conflicts would inevitably occur between those who acquired property and those who had not. Madison agreed with Locke that the primary objective of government is to protect each person's property.

The diversity in the faculties of men, from which the rights of property originate, is not less an insuperable obstacle to a uniformity of interests. The protection of these faculties is the first objective of government.[2]

The US Constitution specifically protects property rights in three separate places. It protects a person's property "against unreasonable searches and seizures;" it allows that no person shall be deprived of "life, liberty or property, without due process of law;" and it prohibits the States from depriving people of "life, liberty or property without due process of law."

The Founders were so concerned about protecting the fruits of one's labor that the US Constitution made it illegal for the federal government to tax a person's income. This prohibition was removed by the 16th Amendment.

With the protection of individual property rights, free markets, low tax rates, and limited government, the United States became the wealthiest and most productive of all the world's major countries.

Why property rights are essential to prosperity

For a nation's workers to be highly productive they must not only have the proper environment...they also need the proper tools. Such tools consist of skills, education, buildings, machines and infrastructure. Infrastructure involves systems that provide for transportation, energy and communications.

The first step in the process of creating wealth involves sacrifice. Individuals must avoid spending all of their income on things that provide current enjoyment. Sacrificing current enjoyment by saving some of our income provides the *potential* for greater satis-faction in the future.

Sacrifice is challenging. Human nature is such that most of us prefer spending our income on things that bring immediate satis-faction. Observe how difficult it is for most children and politi-cians to think of sacrificing today to receive future benefits. And yet, the first step to building for the future involves sacrificing cur-rent enjoyment. When we take a portion of our income and avoid spending it on current enjoyment, those funds are available to spend on those things that are necessary to increase future output.

Risk is the second factor necessary for building wealth. We can never know with certainty what the future holds. Anything can happen. There is always a chance that spending time and money on research, education, machines or anything else designed to pro-vide future enjoyment will end up being a waste of time, effort and money.

In spite of the difficulties in sacrificing and taking risks for future gains, many accept the challenge. Whether the sacrifice and risk is for our families or posterity, most of us have an innate desire to build a better future.

People behave differently. We all know of some who will spend all their money (and more) on current enjoyment regardless of the circumstances. Others will choose to save most of their income regardless of the circumstances. Still others will either take risks or not take them regardless of the likely outcome. These are extremes.

For most of us, incentives dictate how much we will save for the future and the extent we will accept the risks associated with building productive tools. As previously noted, the higher the tax rates on saving and investing, the less people will tend to save and invest. When property rights are not secure it can mean that whatever benefits anyone receives from their sacrifice and risk can be taken away by government. A lack of secure rights to property means that saving and investing can face an effective tax rate of up to 100 percent.

Government cannot compensate for a loss of property rights

The process of creating wealth involves more than saving and investing. It involves specific action and interaction among a nation's most innovative and productive individuals. Innovations produce productive profit opportunities. Entrepreneurs seize these opportunities. They raise the funds necessary to pursue and expand them. At each stage of the process, all those involved respond. They do so in expectation that their actions will produce substantial rewards.

Without property rights there is little incentive for people to sacrifice current enjoyment. Nor will many entrepreneurs undertake the time, effort and risks associated with working for future benefits. The greater the uncertainty surrounding the rights to such benefits, the less likely individuals will be to pursue productive behavior.

Try as they may, government bureaucrats cannot create wealth. Wealth is created by the spontaneous, productive activity of individuals responding to incentives and profit opportunities.

Before its demise, the Soviet Union was notorious for its lack of property rights. Under communism, the State owned almost all property. With such communal arrangements, individuals had little incentive to put money away for the future. Those who did often lost all their savings. Without the promise of ownership, there was little private effort to either save or invest in productive tools.

Saving and investment still occurred. However, it wasn't generated by individuals responding to market pressures. Rather, it was directed by government officials.

State planners knew that directing output toward future use was essential for growth. Hence, Soviet planners dictated how much of current output would be redirected from current enjoyment to creating the tools necessary for future output.

In an effort to generate growth, Soviet planners redirected more than one-third of all the country's output to creating the tools they believed were essential to future growth. This was a larger share of output than in any other country.

In spite of an abundance of forced saving and investment, the Soviet Union turned into the least efficient of the world's major economies. While it allocated massive amounts of resources toward future output, the bulk of these resources were wasted. Without a free market and the incentives associated with entrepreneurial activity, resources were consistently misallocated.

When economic activity responds to the whims and preferences of government bureaucrats instead of the nation's people, wealth tends to be destroyed instead of created.

When everyone owns everything, no one owns anything. While there may be limited communities where altruism and collective ownership of property can survive and thrive, actual examples are few and far between. Too often, human nature takes over. It takes just one slacker to create resentment and spoil the altruism of such communities.

The former Soviet Union violated all of the classical principles, but failing to protect individual property rights was one of its most serious shortcomings. Underground or black markets emerged that enabled people to work and purchase items that were otherwise not available. While these markets can overcome some of the limitations that result from government controls, they are expensive and inefficient.

What cannot be overcome is the lack of private saving and investment. When government fails to protect individual property rights, there is little incentive for rational, industrious individuals either to sacrifice current enjoyment or to take the risks associated with creating wealth.

Soviet planners often pointed out that through government planning they were able to guarantee everyone a job. With an unemployment rate that was reportedly less than one percent, politicians boasted they were the most successful country in the world at creating jobs.

While Soviet workers had jobs, their low productivity meant they also had the lowest living standards of any major economy. In describing their circumstances, Soviet workers had a popular saying: "Our government pretends to pay us, so we pretend to work."

In the US, the Founders insisted that the Constitution protect individuals' property rights. Even so, as constitutional scholar Richard Epstein points out:

...The law of the Constitution is the law of the Supreme Court. Even a cursory examination of its decisions shows a radical disjunction between the private and the public faces of the law. In instance after instance the Court has held state controls to be compatible with the rights of private property. The state can now rise above the rights of the persons whom it represents; it is allowed to assert novel rights that it cannot derive from the persons whom it benefits. Private property once may have been conceived as a barrier to government power, but today that barrier is easily overcome, almost for the asking. [3]

The erosion of property rights can undermine the creation of wealth wherever it occurs. Protecting these rights is crucial for promoting and maintaining a wealthy nation.

People respond to incentives. The greater the potential rewards, the greater the number of individuals who will strive to achieve them. Individuals tend to sacrifice and take risks for future benefits so long as they are convinced they will have control of and benefit from the wealth their actions may produce.

Classical economists view property rights as an essential aspect of individual liberty. They are the key element that helps to motivate individuals to build wealth for the future. When individuals behave in a way that increases their own wealth, they add to the wealth of others.

Individual property rights, free markets, low tax rates and limited government form essential tools that provide the foundation for a wealthy nation.

CHAPTER 11

A Stable Currency

The gold and silver money which circulates in any country may very properly be compared to a highway, which, while it circulates and carries to market all the grass and corn of the country, produces itself not a single pile of either. The judicious operations of banking, by providing, if I may be allowed, so violent a metaphor, a sort of wagon-way through the air; enable the country to convert, as it were, a great part of its highways into good pastures and cornfields, and thereby to increase very considerably the annual produce of its land and labour. The commerce and industry of the country, however, it must be acknowledged, though they may be somewhat augmented, cannot be altogether so secure, when they are thus, as it were, suspended upon the Daedalian wings of paper money, as when they travel about upon the solid ground of gold and silver. –Adam Smith*

Property rights, free markets, low tax burdens and limited government are all essential for generating and sustaining wealth. In order to continually maintain and promote the process individuals also need a currency that accurately reflects the value of what they produce.

The essence of money

Money is essential to economic development. Without money people would have to exchange one specific item for another. Bartering is clumsy and inefficient. Money provides a common medium of exchange for all goods and services. Equally as important, it provides a means for individuals to transfer their buying power from one time period to another.

In a barter economy, it is readily apparent that the income and output associated with each transaction are equal. When a farmer agrees to exchange 10 bushels of corn for a plow, the sale of the corn brings income to the farmer (in the form of a plow). At the same time, the sale of the plow brings income to its producer (in the form of 10 bushels of corn). The income and the sale are two parts of the same transaction. They are obviously equal to each other.

Introducing money into an economy doesn't change the basic nature of transactions. There are always two sides to every transaction. One person's spending is another person's income. Spending and income are two sides of the same coin. They are always equal to each other. Since they are always equal, it follows that all income must be spent in the period it is earned.[1]

This does not mean that each individual has to spend all their income when it is earned. Money allows individuals an easy way to transfer a portion of that income to others. When we put some of our monthly earnings in a bank, or buy stocks or bonds, we transfer that portion of our current claim to this month's output to others. Those who receive this transfer use it to purchase more output than their monthly earnings entitled them to purchase. In return for this privilege, they agree to transfer some of their *future* income to us.

Unlike a barter economy, money provides individuals greater flexibility to transfer their spending power through time. This flexibility allows for the accumulation of wealth, which is an essential feature of all economic development. The introduction of money does not repeal the fact that spending and income must be equal.

Money: good as gold or a politician's promise

Early attempts at creating money used gold and silver as a common means of payment and a store of value over time. Precious metals had the advantage that they had some intrinsic value. The work involved in producing these metals meant that those accepting them for payment had some assurance their value reflected something others had worked to produce. The disadvantage was their use could represent a waste of resources.

Aliens from another planet might find it curious to observe earthlings engaging armies of men and machines to dig gold out of the ground, transport it thousands of miles, only to place it back in the ground.

Early classical economists had mixed feelings regarding the use of gold and silver as money. They recognized the potential waste, but were also leery of the alternative.

The alternative is money that has little or no intrinsic value. Economists refer to such money as *fiat money*. The word *fiat* comes from the Latin meaning "let it be done." It is money because the government says it is money. People tend to accept fiat money in return for their hard earned goods or services because they have faith everyone else will do the same.

At the simplest level, fiat money involves turning something that has negligible value—paper and ink—into something that is accepted in exchange for things people have worked hard to produce. In this sense, fiat money involves creating something of apparent value out of something that has little or no value.

Throughout the world, governments control the creation of money. Almost all use money with no intrinsic value. It is easy to create. The ease of creating it is its main drawback. Politicians and bureaucrats often find it irresistible seemingly to create something out of nothing.

A brief digression into fiscal policy

Fiscal policy refers to the government's use of taxes and spending to influence the economy. *Without the creation of fiat money*, governments face the same constraints as everyone else. In order to buy anything, governments first must acquire the use of income others have earned by creating goods and services. Governments have only two ways to do so. They must either tax or borrow that income from those who earned it.

Many of today's economists believe when government spends money it adds to existing spending and therefore "stimulates" economic activity. To "prove" this point they often draw graphs and write elaborate equations. Some have even built models with water running through tubes to show how adding additional water from a tube labeled "government" increases the flow of water.

Introducing money does not change the basic laws of economics. The spending power earned by a nation's workers stills represents the total claim to the real value of the goods and services they produce. There is no more or less spending power available. Hence, government spending does not add to total spending. All that government spending can do is to *replace* the spending of those who created the goods and services. The suggestion that government spending can somehow add to total spending requires that the same income be spent twice.

To those who believe this is how an economy works, I offer a simple challenge—attempt to spend the income you earn more than once. Buy a government bond with your earnings so the government can spend your money to "stimulate" spending. Then, spend the money you just used to buy the bond on something else. Only after you succeed in spending the same money twice will you have demonstrated how government spending can add to total spending. Fiscal policy is a topic that will be treated more fully in Books II and III of this series.

Money and spending—a simple explanation

The role of money is at the same time one of the simplest and one of the most complex topics in economics. At the simplest level, it is apparent that the ability to create something of apparent value from nothing is analogous to the act of a counterfeiter.

It is easy to imagine what would happen if a counterfeiter set up shop, created money and was able to exchange it for those goods and services other people had worked hard to create.

Initially, as the counterfeiter exchanged his money for goods and services, spending would increase. People would accept the additional money in the belief that it represented a claim to the goods and services produced by others. However, the newly created money reflects no such thing. It represents spending power that was not backed by income earned while creating goods and services.

Income and spending would still equal each other. The counterfeiter's spending would equal his "income" from creating the bogus money. However, since he didn't create anything of substance, the additional spending and income are not backed by any additional goods and services.

If people produced the same amount of goods and services as before the counterfeiter appeared, it would eventually become apparent that the additional money did not reflect the creation of goods and services. Once this occurred, prices would increase to reflect the extra money.

At this point let us assume the counterfeiter is not only caught, but the authorities are able to identify and confiscate all his counterfeit notes, as well. Depending upon how much of the bogus bills each person happened to have, they would find they had less money than they thought. Those who held a large portion of the bogus bills might find they were no longer able to meet their financial obligations to others. If a bank were caught holding a substantial amount of the bogus bills it might fail. The impact of the bank's failure could spread through the community. As the money-induced boom turned to a bust, some might refer to it as a "great recession."

This hypothetical boom and bust is the essence of what occurs when the monetary authorities create either too much or too little money to support a normal flow of business. Ideally, a nation needs a specific amount of money to support its creation of goods and services. An economy that is growing rapidly can use more money each year to support its increase in goods and services. One that is not growing would not need additional money.

Since creating fiat money is so cheap and easy, it is far more likely that the politicians and bureaucrats who control the process will produce more money each year than the actual increase in goods and services. Doing so sends prices higher, eroding the value of money.

Money and spending—some complexities

The simple monetary explanation for booms and busts, as well as for inflation and deflation, is essentially what occurs. The details associated with this process involve a number of complicating factors.

When governments create more fiat money they create the means to increase spending and income, but they do so without the creation of more goods and services. As in the case of the counterfeiter, spending will tend to increase. Whether or not this will increase the production of goods and services depends on the situation.

If an economy already has an adequate amount of money so workers are fully employed, the additional money will raise prices. However, if there is excess capacity and unemployed workers, the additional money and spending can serve to increase real output.

There are a number of other areas where the introduction of money can cause confusion. The process by which central banks create money is one of those areas. The impact of a fractional reserve banking system and precisely what constitutes money and who should control it are others. The desirability of using gold for money and the value of one country's currency relative to others are still other complicating factors.

All of the factors related to money and monetary policy are potentially so confusing they are often misunderstood, even by those in charge of the process. If money were easily understood, most of the booms and busts in the economy would have been avoided and the words inflation and deflation would seldom be mentioned.

A complete treatment of the complexities involved in monetary and fiscal policy and the impact they have on the economy is beyond the scope of this chapter. For now, the main point is that monetary stability is important in promoting a stable business climate. Without such stability, efforts to generate wealth will be marked by alternating periods of booms and busts. Such periods clearly undermine efforts to promote the wealth of nations.

CHAPTER 12

Summing Up Book I

I predict future happiness for Americans if they can prevent the government from wasting the labors of the people under the pretense of taking care of them. –Thomas Jefferson

Early classical economists focused on a specific goal—identify policies that would generate and sustain growth to enhance the material well-being of most individuals. These economists identified essential principles that would accomplish this objective. The principles are free markets, low tax rates and limited government, property rights and a stable currency. These principles encourage individuals to work diligently, plan for the future and prosper.

Not all individuals were expected to behave in this manner. Human nature dictates that some would always behave irresponsibly. They would seek an easy life, relaxing and avoiding productive activity. With little regard for the future, some would spend money foolishly. Others would behave prudently regardless of circumstances.

Each nation will always have its share of underachievers and over-achievers. Economic success isn't an accident. It depends on creating conditions that encourage the largest possible number of individuals to make prudent choices.

Classical economists believe their principles promote responsible, constructive behavior among most of a nation's people. By freely responding to market forces, individuals would provide the necessary means to generate and sustain growth.

Creative people would determine how to do things better. Entrepreneurs would find that savers would readily provide the resources necessary for them to build and expand on ways to produce more and better goods and services. Innovations in one area would spawn those in others. A virtuous cycle of successful innovation would then produce many relatively prosperous individuals and hence, wealthy nations.

Those whose behavior was the most instrumental in increasing that wealth would tend to gain the greatest financial rewards. However, as a nation's efficiency increased, so would the living standards of most of its people. As a result, even those who failed to sacrifice, acquire skills or pursue the risks involved in creating wealth would tend to find their living standards had also improved.

Nations that followed classical principles would tend to see innovations promote efficiency and minimize waste. The greater the growth and the longer it continued, the more a nation would prosper.

Ultimately, if the process continued long enough, and without too many diversions, a typical worker would end up producing a substantial amount of goods and services each year and reaping the benefits associated with a wealthy nation.

The more we examine the logic of the early classical economists, the more apparent it becomes that their ideas are not only reasonable...at their core they distill to common sense.

Previous chapters provided examples of the harm that often occurs when policymakers abandon classical principles. Those examples merely scratch the surface. There have been stark differences between the performance of countries that have heeded classical economists and those that have not. The next book in this series deals with these differences.

After more than two centuries of experimentation, the evidence is overwhelming. It leads to an obvious conclusion—early classical economists were correct. Classical economic principles provide the necessary means for unleashing the wealth of nations.

Footnotes

Footnotes

Chapter 1: Origins of Classical Thought

1. (Locke 1690, New Edition 1824)

2. (Sowell 2006) pp. 17-19.

Chapter 3: Free Markets

1. (Read 1958)

2. (Smith 1937 {First edition published 1776)) p. 423.

Chapter 4: Objections to Free Markets I

1. (Goldberg 2007) p. 264.

2. Department of Labor; classicalprinciples.com

3. (Vedder 1993, 1997) pp. 8-9.

4. Ibid. p. 9.

5. Alternative approaches to help low wage workers can be found in Chapter 9.

Chapter 5: Objections to Free Markets II

1. (Timiraos 2010)

2. (Dash 2008)

3. Data and calculations by the author are at classicalprinciples.com

4. (Sowell 2004)

Chapter 6: Low Tax Rates

1. (Smith 1937 (First edition published 1776)) pp. 778-779.

2. Ibid., p. 718.

Chapter 7: Limited Government
1. (Machan 1995) p. 153.

Chapter 8: Government Failure

1. (J. E. Stiglitz 71(1981)) (J. E. Stiglitz June, 1986) (Cowen 2002)

2. (Hopkins 1996) (de Rugy 2009) (R. J. Genetski 1997)

3. (Genetski 1997)

4. (Johnston 2007)

5. (CBO 2010)

6. (Timiraos 2010)

7. (Foley & Lardner 2005) (Financial Executives Institute 2008) (classicalprinciples.com)

8. (Kotz 2009)

9. (Wall Street Journal Editorial 2010)

10. (Urbina 2010)

11. (Neil and Johnson 2010)

Chapter 9: Government's Role in Creating Wealth

1. (C. A. Murray 1984)

2. (C. Murray 2006)

3. (Locke 1690, New Edition 1824) p. 215.

Chapter 10: Property Rights

1. (Locke 1690, New Edition 1824) p. 204.

2. (Hamilton, et al. 1961) p. 130-131.

3. (Epstein 1985) pp. ix-x.

Chapter 11: A Stable Currency

1. This point is far from obvious. The failure to grasp it has generated a great deal of confusion throughout the history of economics. One seemingly obvious objection is the odd occurrence of a person who receives income but decides to bury the money in his or her back yard. (Such behavior is similar to our farmer burying the plow he received for his corn instead of using it.) The buried money still represents income to the person in the time period it was earned as well as spending on the part of the person that provided the income. The fact the income won't be used by its recipient (or put in the bank so someone else will use it) means the next round of spending and income generation will be delayed by such odd behavior. If the money were to stay in the ground, the net effect of such an action would be to reduce the amount of money in circulation thereby increasing the value of the money that remains in circulation.

It took classical economist Irving Fisher two volumes of detailed analysis and explanation to provide a full treatment of this topic. Those interested in pursuing these issues can do so in the following references. (Fisher, The Nature of Capital and Income 1906 (1930)) (Fisher, The Rate of Interest 1907 (1982))

Chapter 12 Summing Up Book I

An extensive analysis of the evidence is presented in Book II of this series (Genetski upcoming). An excellent summary of the evidence can also be found in (Powell 2008).

Bibliography

Brown, Sherrod. *Myths of Free Trade*. New York: The New Press, 2004.

Brunner, Robert F. *The Dynamics of a Financial Crisis: The Panic of 1907 and the Subprime Crisis*. Working Paper, http://papers.ssrn.com/sol3/papers.cfm?abstract_id=1434714, 2009.

CBO. *CBO's Budgetary Treatment of Fannie Mae and Freddie Mac*. Washington, DC: The Congress of the United States, 2010.

Cowen, Tyler & Crampton, Eric. *Market Failure or Success The New Debate*. Chletenham UK: The Independent Institute, 2002.

Dash, Eric. "Former Executives at Fannie and Freddie Stand to Collect Big Paychecks." *New York Times*, September 8, 2008.

de Rugy, Veronique and Warren, Melinda. *Regulators' Budget 31*. St. Louis: Washington University in St. Louis; Weidenbaum Center on the Economy, Government and Public Policy, 2009.

Dobbs, Lou. *Exporting America*. New York: Warner Books, 2004.

Epstein, Richard A. *Takings*. Cambridge, Massachusetts: Harvard University Press, 1985.

Fisher, Irving. *The Nature of Capital and Income*. New York: The Macmillan Company, 1906 (1930).

—. *The Rate of Interest*. New York: Macmillan (Garland Publishing), 1907 (1982).

Foley & Lardner. *SOX's Section 404 Hits Hard: Average Audit Fees for Small Companies Increased 96 percent to $1 million in FY 2004*. Foley & Lardner, June 16, 2005.

Genetski, Robert. *Classical Economic Principles & the Wealth of Nations: Book II.* upcoming.

—. *Classical Economic Principles and the Wealth of Nations: Book III.* upcoming.

Genetski, Robert J. *A Nation of Millionaires.* Lanham New York Oxford: Madison Books, 1997.

—. *Taking the Voodoo Out of Economics.* Lake Bluff, Illinois: Regnery Books, 1986.

—. *classicalprinciples.com*

Goldberg, Jonah. *Liberal Fascism.* New York: Broadway Books, 2007.

Hamilton, Alexander, Madison James, Jay John, and edited by Benjamin F. Wright. *The Federalist.* New York: Barnes & Noble, 1961.

Hopkins, Thomas D. *Regulatory Costs in Profile.* St. Louis: Center for the Study of American Business, 1996.

Houghton, Jonathan and Khandker, Shahidur R. *Handbook on Poverty and Inequality.* Washington, DC: The World Bank, 2009.

Institute, Financial Executives. *FEI Survey: Average 2007 SOX Compliance Cost $1.7 Million.* Financial Executives Institute, April 30, 2008.

Iversen, Carl. *International Capital Movements.* New York: Augustus M. Kelley, 1935 (1967).

Johnson, Neil King JR. and Keith. "BP Relied on Faulty US Data." *The Wall Street Journal,* June 24, 2010: 1.

Johnston, David Cay. *Free Lunch.* New York: Penguin Group, 2007.

Kotz, H. David. *Investigation of Failure of the SEC to Uncover Bernie Madoff's Ponzi Scheme: Case No. OIG-509.* Report of Investigation, Office of Inspector General, 2009.

Krugman, Paul. *The Conscience of a Libersl.* New York: W.W. Norton & Co., 2007.

Locke, John. *Two Treatises on Government.* London : C. Baldwin, Printer (books.google.com, 1690, New Edition 1824.

Machan, Tibor. *Private Rights & Public Illusions.* New Brunswick, New Jersey: Transaction Publishers; The Independence Institute, 1995.

Murray, Charles A. *Losing Ground: American Social Policy 1950-1980.* New York: Basic Books, 1984.

Murray, Charles. *In Our Hands: A Plan to Replace the Welfare State.* Washington, DC: American Enterprise Institute, 2006.

Neil, King Jr., and Keith Johnson. "BP Relied on Faulty US Data." *The Wall Street Journal*, June 24, 2010: 1.

Powell, Benjamin (editor). *Making Poor Nations Rich.* Stanford, CA: Stanford University Press, 2008.

Powell, Jim. "John Locke Natural Rights to Life, Liberty and Property." *Freeman: Ideas on Liberty*, August 1996.

Read, Leonard E. "I, Pencil." essay, 1958.

Smith, Adam. *An Inquiry into the Nature and causes of The Wealth of Nations.* New York: The Modern Library, 1937 (First edition published 1776).

Sowell, Thomas. "Price Gouging in Florida." *Jewish World Review,* September 14, 2004.

—. *On Classical Economics.* New Haven & London: Yale University Press, 2006.

Stiglitz, Joseph E. & Weiss, Andrew. "Credit Rationing In Markets With Imperfect Information." *American Economic Review,* 71(1981): 393-410.

Stiglitz, Joseph E. *Theories of Wage Rigidity.* NBER Working Paper No. 1442, National Bureau of Economic Research, June, 1986.

Timiraos, Nick. "S&P: Fannie, Freddie Overhaul Could Cost $685 Billion." *Wall Street Journal,* October 4, 2010.

Urbina, Ian. *The New York Times,* June 6, 2010: A1.

Vedder, Richard K. and Gallaway, Lowell E. *Out of Work: Unemployment and Government in Twentieth Century America (updated edition).* New York and London: The Independent Institute, 1993, 1997.

Wall Street Journal Editorial. "The Uncertainty Principle—II." *The Wall Street Journal,* July 16, 2010.

WSJ editorial. "The New Cannery Row." *The Wall Street Journal,* June 1, 2010.